10 Ways To Make More Money For The Single Daddy

Simple Money Making Ideas For The Busy Single Dad

Nick Thomas

Copyright © 2015 Nick Thomas

All rights reserved

No part of this book may be reproduced in any form or by any electronic or mechanical means including information storage and retrieval systems, without permission in writing from the author. The only exception is by a reviewer, who may quote short excepts in a review.

Although the author and publisher have made every effort to ensure that the information in this book was correct at press time, the author and publisher do not assume and hereby disclaim any liability to any party for any loss, damage, or disruption caused by errors or omissions, whether such errors or omissions result from negligence, accident, or any other cause.

Visit my website at www.singledaddydating.com

ISBN-13: 978-1505405491

ISBN-10: 1505405491

JOIN OUR COMMUNITY!

Single Daddy Dating is a growing community of single fathers who look to help each other, not only with dating success but in all areas of their lives too. This includes parenting, career and finances advice.

Join us today and get '**10 Crucial Checklist To Dating Success For Single Fathers**' completely FREE!

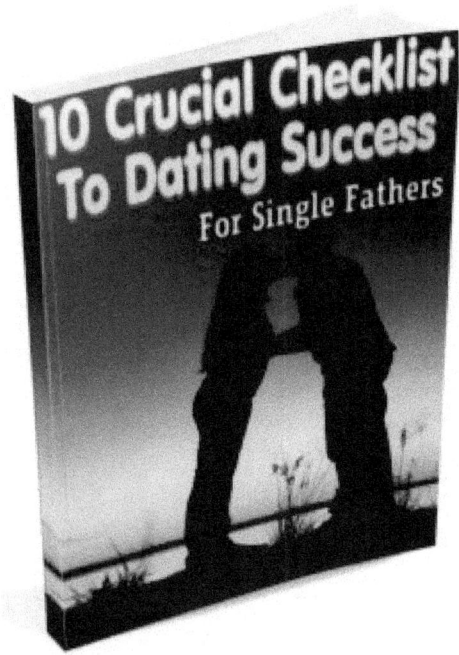

JOIN US AT
WWW.SINGLEDADDYDATING.COM/NEWSLETTER/

NICK THOMAS www.singledaddydating.com

10 WAYS TO MAKE MORE MONEY

CONTENTS

Chapter 1 – Making More Money As A Single Father .. 1

Chapter 2 – Is Money What You Need?.......................... 7

Chapter 3 – Learn To Manage Your Money First 11

Chapter 4 – A New Economy: Making Money From Home 14

Chapter 5 – Popular Methods For Single Fathers To Make Money Online 19

Chapter 6 – Sell Your Time.. 29

Chapter 7 – Weird Ways To Make More Money 37

Chapter 8 – Having A "Business" Mindset 42

Chapter 9 – Extra Business Ideas For Single Fathers ... 47

Final Notes.. 52

Chapter 1: Making More Money As A Single Father

A divorce puts many men in difficult financial situations. For George, it was something that changed his life altogether. He had the difficulty of paying alimony and needed to pay the mortgage on the house. Together, those two payments bothered him. He needed more money and looked to save as much money as possible from his job.

He ate instant noodles and other cheap microwaveable food and thought of every way possible to save more money. He might have save some money, but it only cost him in different ways. He started to gain weight – 30 pounds to be exact and was sick all the time. He saved money on his food but he needed to spend more money on seeing the doctor. His visits to the doctor were so frequent he knew he needed to do something.

As much as he wanted to save money on food, he knew he needed to completely overhaul his diet and lifestyle. He needed to stop thinking so much about saving money and to focus on making more money.

Many single fathers like George are looking for avenues to make more money. Due to difficult times, coupled with the stresses of alimony and mortgage, many single fathers seek for alternatives outside their 9-5 jobs. It is not only those 'big' expenses that can drag a single father down financially, but also the other 'smaller' expenses like food, utility bills and children's expenses which can add up.

The thing about saving is that there is only a limited amount of money which you can save. For example, if you make $5,000 a month and you currently spend a total of $4,000 a month on your mortgage, alimony and other expenses. What's the maximum you can save?

$4,000

That's the maximum, although realistically speaking, you would never save that much. You can't expect to be homeless and forgo your alimony payments. Even that, you need to spend on gas to get to work. Surely that's an expense.

Now think differently.

How much can you MAKE?

Unlimited. **The money you can make is unlimited while the money you can save is always limited.** Do you understand why you need to start thinking about making more money?

This is the main reason for this book. It is to teach single fathers ways of making more money. There are plenty of reasons to make more money. Everyone could give themselves reasons for wanting to make more money.

For a single father, it may be to:-

- Deal with their monthly expenses better
- Save for retirement
- Save for children's college fund
- Children's pocket money
- For a goal in the future (like travelling)
- For a rainy day

All these are solid reasons for a single father to make more money. However, the other main question to ask is:-

Do you have time to make more money?

That's a big factor. What's the point of knowing all the methods of making more money if you don't have the point to pursue them? You need to see how much time you have to start a new venture or new part time job.

Firstly, you need to consider the time that you have after your work, parenting responsibilities etc. Write down how much time you have. Think about how many hours you have each week to start off a venture.

For certain ventures, you can even involve your children. They have a lot of free time and they can help you. Different single fathers have different resources. You would need to think thoroughly about what resources you have and be creative with them.

I can share with you all the methods of making more money, but you would have to be creative and seek even better ways to make money.

When it comes to making more money as a single father, I truly believe that there are an abundance of ways to make more money. However, you need to first learn to manage your time better. As you start to manage your time better, you would have more time to dedicate to making more money.

But wait, I have yet to ask you a very important question, which is…

Chapter 2: Is Money What You Need?

Is money what you need?

When I ask this to many single fathers, I would tend to get this response:

"Of course I need more money. What the hell are you talking about, Nick. Who doesn't need more money?"

Sometimes, you need to understand the true reasons why you want to make more money. Is money what you really need?

The thing for many people is that they

confuse their needs with their wants. Look deeply into their expenses and you see that they have many unnecessary expenses which simply cripple them. They buy plenty of things they don't need and spend so much time paying for them. I have known people who pay almost $200 a month for magazine subscription but barely read those magazines.

Why do you need to make more money then? To pay for more things you don't need?

That's the vicious cycle that many people put themselves under. They look to make more money, but don't have a real specific purpose for it. Beneath those expenses they have, they don't take time to spend on things that truly matter in life.

If you realize that your life is filled with many unnecessary junk that you don't need, you need to look to downsize your life first. Try to remove the unnecessary expenses in your life which simply weights you down. As you simplify your life, you would be able to deal with your finances better.

Through simplification of your life, you can focus on what's essential. This focus is important because it gives you a better opportunity to make more money. If your expenses is filled with things that don't create any value in your life, how do you expect to advance and make more money?

You can start the process of simplifying your expenses by thinking about your priorities in life. For single fathers, their priorities would normally be their children and making ends meet. Are your expenses reflective of that? Or do you have many "mindless expenses"

After that, you need to write down those expenses that you have and prioritize them. Eliminate those expenses that aren't creating substantial value in your life. Spend money only on those that are important.

During the process of making more money, you need to have a laser-like focus. By having this laser-like focus, you have made an important first step towards making more money and living a different life in the future.

After simplifying your life, you have an opportunity. In the next chapter, you would learn about one of the greatest way of making money in the past ten years…

Chapter 3: Learn To Manage Your Money First

Making money is important, but what's more important is learning how to manage your money. There are many people out there who make good money but struggle to save it. There are some wealthy business people I know who make more than $5million each year, but spend $7million.

For you, it can be hard to imagine. How the hell does one person spend $7million?

Trust me, it's possible. This is because there

isn't any limit to how much you can spend. Even if you make multiple billions each year, it would be useless if you lack the money management skills. That is why money management is important. It ensures that you don't spend too much and end up in debt.

When it comes to managing your money, you need to focus on spending money on what's important. I have already gone in depth about this in the previous chapter.

However, what makes money management easier is when you automate it. You can do this by setting up a standing order in your bank. The moment your salary comes in each month, money would be transferred to another account (as a savings). This is just an example of automating your money.

When you learn to manage your money well, you can slowly become financially well-off. Your savings can provide you a fund to start up a business or give you a cushion while you change to a more fulfilling job.

As such, you can't simply depend on making more money. You still need to keep track of your finances before you start on a new venture to make more money. In the future when you have made more money, you still need to have a strategy to save and grow it.

Making more money doesn't give you the license to spend more money. Rather it is about having a list of spending priorities to make your life easier.

Chapter 4: A New Economy - Making Money From Home

I love being in this time in history. I love the fact that we are being in this era of technology where everything is so easy. Where we can simply make money from the comfort of home. Nowadays, I make money from home. I have several internet businesses that have really changed my life for the better.

Only a few decades ago, this would be

unimaginable. People used to travel a few hours a day just to get to work. Some would move to the city to find for jobs. They would leave their family just to make a living.

But things have changed now. I have heard of people moving away from the city because they are able to work remotely. Gone were the days where you need to spend so much time commuting to work all the time.

By working from home, you wouldn't need to spend time and money travelling to and from work. You don't have to buy a car and you can choose to work flexibly. This feature of working from home really suits a single father who has parental responsibilities. If you have younger children who need you, working from home allows you to fulfil those responsibilities much easier.

With a simple computer and access to internet, you can make good money from home. Although it is easier said than done, it still represents a good opportunity. I am not guaranteeing that you would succeed in making money online immediately but I'm telling you that there are tons of opportunities online.

However, what this represents is a great chance for you to build a business that allows you the freedom. This is provided you take the time to learn what is needed and have the patience to succeed. Making money online takes time.

I have known many people who succeed at making money online. In my single father support group meetings, I normally give advice to some single fathers who have online businesses. Some of them use these online platform for retail purposes while some use them to sell their services.

Simply put, there are many ways of making money online, which will be covered in the next chapter.

If you are keep to make money online, you need to learn that there are some basic principles if you want to succeed. These basic principles are important regardless of what business you choose to enter in. Business in general are guided by some basic rules which are evergreen:-

- **Trust.** If you want to start a business, you need to understand the value of trust. Trust is the fundamental component of all relationships worth having. Without trust, you wouldn't have any quality relationships. In business, relationships are the key. When setting up a business, make sure that trust becomes an integral part of your dealings with others.

- **Value.** Businesses that succeed are those that provide value to the customer. It can't get any simpler. If you want to succeed in business, you need to understand what the customers' needs and the problems are.

Make sure that you have a clear value proposition that would help the end user.

- **Integrity.** Integrity is about being honest. It is about doing what you say you will do. It is an important part of having trust in doing business. Businesses with integrity are those that stay for the long term. If you want to build something that lasts, you need to develop a habit of integrity.

For some people who are in employment, it can be difficult for them to understand why I relate these factors to business all the time.

This is because making money from home IS a business. Even if you decide to be a freelance writer or graphics designer, you are already in business. By upholding to this few key principles, making money online becomes much easier.

Chapter 5: Popular Methods For Single Fathers To Make Money Online

In this chapter, you would find 7 popular methods to make money online. The benefits of these methods is that there are legitimate business methods which you can start during your free time. Some would require more time while some would require less.

It really depends on what skills you have, how much time you have and whether you are interested in having a business like that. You would need to take time to learn about these different methods in depth so you know whether you would want to pursue it over the long term.

Remember, for any business to be successful, you need to have a substantial time investment. You need to put in time to lay down the foundations of your business.

Work Freelance

There are many online work which you can apply for on a freelance basis. The recession that happened in 2008 has greatly changed the economy. Companies are looking for more contract and freelance work as opposed to hiring full-time workers.

The reason for this is simple: It saves costs.

For businesses to have full time workers, they

need to pay the workers benefits, a full time pay (even if they aren't productive) and have an office for them. Farming out work makes more sense for companies because the company can pay for the work that they need done instead of paying workers a fixed salary regardless of whether there is work or not.

According to a research done, 9 out of 10 companies are using at least some kind of contract work to get things done. If you have certain skills like writing, graphic design, web design or editing; you can use them to your benefits.

The pay for freelance work is higher than for salaried positions, based on a per hour basis. This is because you would need to pay for your own expenses like your laptop, electricity bill at home and other things that would impact the quality of work. Most of them are already a 'sunk cost' for you. This means that you have already paid for them.

To search for such work, you can head to places like eLance, oDesk and Freelancer. These are all top freelance marketplace.

For a better understanding of creating a freelance business, check out…

www.singledaddydating.com/freelance

Affiliate Marketing

This online making method is perhaps the most popular. I have used it to make good money and perhaps you have already heard about it.

Affiliate marketing is simply promoting a certain product online. From there, you get a cut of the commission should someone purchases the product from your link. You can promote anything online and then get a cut from it.

It is as simple as that. It is not within the

confinements of this book to teach you the basics of affiliate marketing because it is a very diverse field with various strategies involved. A better place is a free educational website at

www.singledaddydating.com/affiliatemarketing

Become An eBay Power Seller

eBay is one of the biggest buying and selling platform. Many people are already aware of how easy is it to use eBay, whether you are buying or selling. You might already be buying loads of stuffs from there.

Why not start to make some money from there now?

Open up a store and become a power seller. You can sell anything you want. You may start off small, but once you are established, you can start to scale it up.

You can source for things from China and sell

it wherever you are.

Be A Dropshipper

Dropshipping is similar to affiliate marketing. You simply promote a product without needing to carry any inventory.

It can't get simpler than that.

However, you would need to learn how to drive traffic and look for quality products to sell. Don't ever sell low quality products if you want to succeed. Remember, trust is very important in business. This is more so for online businesses where your reputation is everything.

I have known some people who have interests in a certain hobbies and start using this business model to make more money. This guy Dave started to sell fishing rods due to his interest in fishing.

He simply created a website and started to sell fishing rods. Best thing is, he didn't have to keep any inventory of fishing rods. He simply write articles about fishing and garnered a following. His followers would buy those fishing rods that he recommends and he has built a steady business from this method.

Online Media Consultant

This method requires a lot of time upfront and an interest in certain topic. It would be suitable if you are someone who like participating on forums, social media and so on.

You can be an online media consultant and help other people/businesses promote things. You can start small by helping local businesses get a presence on social media and helping them generate some content.

From there, you can also develop a website

for them if you have those skills. In fact, those skills can be easily learned if you have the time. I have known a single father who manages to create a simple website for companies at $350 each. He manages to make around 3 websites each week. That's more than $4k each month.

These small businesses require an online presence to grow their business. Learning the ins and outs of social media and building an audience helps them tremendously in the business.

Virtual Assistant

Many busy people seek to have someone who can help check their email and plan their daily schedules. If you have time to do such things, becoming a virtual assistant is a method of making good money.

With a stable internet connection, you can

easily do this. Among the tasks that a virtual assistant can do include planning appointment, data entry, basic bookkeeping, research and many more. If you have any of those skills, you can easily start off as a virtual assistant.

www.singledaddydating.com/virtualassistant/

Sell eBooks

If you have a knack for writing, you can sell eBooks online. Write about a topic you are interested in and look to sell them online. These eBooks are great tools to promote your other services too, if you have them.

Ebooks isn't only about writing them. You also need to learn how to format, publish and market them. It can be a very lucrative business to be in because you only need to write those books once and the income would come in all the time, provided you choose the right topics to write about and you are doing constant marketing.

Chapter 6: Sell Your Time

For some single fathers, they would be better off selling their time because they aren't keen to start something online. Although making money online can be a great way to make more money, it is something that can be challenging for those people who don't feel comfortable using computers all the time.

Fret not, there are also plenty of other ways for single fathers to make money. Although online income is a great way, you can also make a good living by selling your time. There are many people who need certain services but can't because they are too busy. Many of this services required can be easy to provide. However, it would still depends on your interests and resources that you have.

Work At Starbucks

I know a single father who works in Starbucks on a part time basis. Truth is, that was what he did to build up his online business. He would work in Starbucks for 20 hours each week and then spend another 20 hours each week to build his online business.

Even for part time workers, Starbucks offer an impressive range of benefits to its employees. Among the benefits include comprehensive health, dental and vision insurance. Besides that, paid vacation is even provided for half-time employees. There are many other benefits that Starbucks provides too.

No wonder they are constantly rated as one of the top 100 companies to work for by Fortune Magazine.

For single fathers, working in a Starbuck might not make them much money. But, if you treat working as Starbucks as a stop-gap while you build something else, it can give you tremendous benefits over the long term.

Staffing For Special Events Or Conventions

Whenever there are special events or trade conventions, it would be a good opportunity for companies to market their products. To do this, they would need local people to work for them. The job scope may include attracting attention to the booth and sending out flyers.

The company might decide to promote a new cell phone or send out certain samples of a new soda outside a concert venue. The company may ask you to wear their T-Shirt as you look to promote their products. Commonly, the pay is hourly or on a whole day basis.

To apply for such jobs, you need to send your resume, headshot and physical description to such companies. Never underestimate such jobs. It may take up a weekend but the money can be quite good. I have known people who make up to $200 a day just doing such things.

Become A Dog Walker

There are many people who have dogs but simply don't have the time to walk them. Some don't walk their dogs because they don't like walking in the first place. They think of walking their dogs as a hassle.

Dog walking as a business has really become more popular in recent years. You can offer them a solution by walking their dogs. It represents a wonderful solution for them. This can easily bring in $10 per hour. Find for three or four dogs and you have $40. Not bad for an hour's work.

Be organized with your time and you can easily make $100 each day from walking dogs alone.

Exercise Teacher

There are some gyms that are willing to trade memberships and a bit more for people who have the skills to teach an exercise class. Offer your services to the gym and see what classes you can teach. These gyms won't offer only their memberships but have good salaries as well, if you can put in more hours.

You can also become a personal trainer to those people who don't go to the gym. If you are someone who is in good shape and knows how to teach people to build their fitness, this is definitely a great money making idea. If you slowly build up a reputation of helping others get results, your income would slowly grow.

Handy Man Repairs

If you are skilled with basic home repair, you can perform this services for a pretty lucrative income. Let other people know that you have these skills and ask them to call you if they have any repair jobs like plumbing, electrical work and painting the house.

You would be amazed by the amount of money people are willing to pay to solve these problems. Even if you aren't skilled at these basic home repairs, you can always take time to learn. With the convenience of the internet and YouTube, you can easily learn many of these basic skills.

Senior Citizen Assistance

There are many elderly people who need help with a wide variety of tasks in their day to day lives. This may include simple tasks such as laundry, cleaning and taking a shower. It may seem simple to you, but it would be very difficult for them to do it themselves.

Many children of these elderly people are more than willing to hire someone responsible and close to the proximity to help out their parents. It not only allows you to make a good income from helping out these senior citizens, it also allows you to make a good income from it.

Tutoring

If you are a major in a particular topic in college or have skills with children, tutoring is another great way of making money. Having the knowledge to teach is something very lucrative if you use it well. Seek out parents who are willing to pay for your services. Provide quality materials to them.

You can market your services online or by passing out flyers. Besides that, you can also promote your services in single parent groups. These parents would be more than willing to pay for your services if you can guide their children to do better in school.

Chapter 7: Weird Ways To Make More Money

In the previous two chapters, I have shared many ways of making more money. Some of them are more obvious while some aren't. Some require more skills while some don't.

In this chapter, you would learn about various weird ways of making more money. Some of these methods are plain WEIRD. You may have trouble believing that some of them are actual money-making methods. Some are simply quick method of generating a quick sum of money.

Sell Your Gold Jewellery

The previous recession has drove the price of gold commodity through the roof. The price of gold has reached an all-time high in 2010. As such, it is a perfect time to unload old or broken gold jewelry that you aren't using anymore. Or you can wait until you feel until the price is right before selling it.

Head to a local jewelry and see how much your gold jewelry is worth. See if the price he offers is near to what you are expecting. This 'money-making' method doesn't really require skills, but desperate times call for desperate measures. Perhaps you have some old jewelry left by your parents that you simply have no use for anymore.

Become A Mystery Shopper

Mystery shoppers are people paid by market research companies to report on their retail experiences. This may be like shopping, eating in restaurants and buying gas. For each task, they would give you specific instructions such as what to look for, what to do and where to shop.

From there, you would report back how your experience went. This includes the customer service, employee attitudes and cleanliness of facilities. Once you submit your report, you would be paid a sum of money. This money covers a fee for your time and reimbursement for anything you have bought.

Sell Your Sperm

Yes. Selling your sperm is a viable way of making more money. While some people may be uncomfortable with giving away their genetic material, some won't even be bothered. It is in fact a very profitable 'venture'.

Sperm donors get between $50 and $100 for

each donation. Different sperm banks have different criteria before you donate. They would check that your health is alright and that you are of a certain height. There are some which even require a degree or high school diploma. You won't believe the weird requirements that these sperm banks have!

Become A Test Subject For A NASA Bed Rest Study

It may seem too good to be true, but NASA pays you $5,000 to lie in bed for 90 days. These experiments have scientific purposes. Test subjects would lie with their legs elevated to mirror what astronauts experience in space. Subjects aren't allowed to engage in much physical activity but they can watch TV or use computers.

This money making venture may be difficult for a single father if he doesn't have much time. You can't expect to be a 'part-time' test subject for such ventures. But, if you do have the time, this is definitely something you can try.

Sign Up For A Medical Trial

Pharmaceutical companies are always looking for individuals to test new drugs that are brought into the market. This is where you can make some money from. If you agree to such tests, you can make up to $3000 per study.

Disclaimer though. There would be some possible side effects, and you would need to pick a study that accommodates your day job. Those side effects need to be evaluated before you take on those tests. It isn't worth the money if you end up feeling sickly after that.

Chapter 8: Having A "Business" Mindset

Except for the 'weird' ways of making money in the previous chapters, it always pay to have a business mindset in whatever you do.

Whether you are seeking for ways to make money online or sell your time, having a business mindset allows you to increase the money you make. You need to think of ways to increase your income, manage your expenses and even have some personal "Research and Development" or "R&D".

"R&D" is important if you are starting a business. You would want to be constantly improving yourself if you are in business. You want to improve so you can provide more value to others. Every business in existence would look to improve themselves all the time.

The company you work for may send you for many training. The reason for this? So you can improve yourself. This is the same for you if you are starting a business on your own. You need to take the time to learn more things, be it from books or online.

From the online world, you can learn many things that are free or low-cost. From graphic design, building websites, business skills or internet marketing; these are all valuable skills that can give you a side income as a single father.

Although all those skills can help you one way or another, these are among the business skills that you should have. It doesn't matter what kind of 'business' you are in, these are imperative to your success in making more money:

- **Marketing Skills.** Many people have great skills but have problems getting people who are willing to pay for those skills. The main reason? They lack the marketing skills to market their services. As such, they are unable to capitalise on such a situation. Learn some marketing skills like how to write copy or sell yourself online. These skills allow you to promote your services, even if you charge a premium for them.

- **Networking.** It isn't enough for you to market your services. You still need to learn some networking skills to grow your business. This means that you need to get out of the house and meet new people who can help you. Find for networking events around your local area and mingle around with other people. Single parent support groups are another great place for single fathers. During these networking events, look to share some notes and tell other people what you do.

- **Basic Accounting.** Accounting is perhaps the most underrated subject in business. It is so important that many people simply neglect to take time to learn it properly. You need to understand the basics of accounting such as income/expenditure and asset/liabilities. It will help you to manage your finances better while you build your business.

- **Constant Improvement.** It is worth mentioning again the importance of "R&D". Without constantly improving yourself, your business would stagnant. Take time off to learn new skills all the time. These skills would do a lot of good for the future of your business. Think of a long term vision for your venture. What skills would you need to have to make that vision come true?

Having a business mindset helps elevate your business in no time at all. Stop thinking of yourself merely as an 'employee' if you want to make more money.

As you start to develop a 'business' mindset, you would be able to provide more value to your customers. Even if you are an employee in a company, having a business mindset allows you to bring more value to the company. You would be more appreciated and brings you more career advancement.

Chapter 9: Extra Business Ideas For Single Fathers

I have shared plenty of money making ideas, but there are more. In this chapter, you would learn about various extra money making ideas that are easy and won't take too much time.

Cover Your Car With Advertisment

Have you seen those cars down the road with many plastered ads for energy drinks or snacks?

You may have thought that those cars belong to company or its employees, but it isn't. Instead, many advertisement firms are willing to pay drivers to have their cars covered with ads.

Depending on the company, length of promotion, product and your location; you can easily earn up to $1000 a month to serve as a moving billboard. All you need to do is to simply sign up on the company's website, fill in the basic information and they would contact you.

Some promotion last only a few months while some could last up to a year. Think of it, it would be a great income for something that you don't have to do anything extra. They would do the sticking of advertisement of the car and removal in the future, leaving your car totally undamaged.

Be An Agent For A Direct Selling Company

Direct selling companies use individual salespeople to sell their products instead of using traditional retail methods. These direct selling companies such as Avon and Amway, have a long history of direct selling.

Simply sign up with one of the company's salesperson and you are in business. If you have the charisma of a quality salesperson, this direct selling method can make you good money. If not, you would want to give this method a miss. You would only lose friends in the long term.

Rent Out A Spare Room In Your House

If you happen to have a spare room at home, you can look to rent out the room to make easy money on the side. Depending on the market for rentals in your area, you can easily make $250 to $600 each month from renting out a room.

Check the newspaper classified to see the rental in your area. You can also check AirBnB.com.

However, renting isn't as easy as it is. It is not about sitting back and collecting the money. There are many other tasks involved such as drawing up a lease, finding a tenant and even managing the tenant. Before renting out your place, you also need to do a check on the local legislation to see if you can rent out your place.

Bed And Breakfast

If you have extra space, you can even have a bed and breakfast. This is similar to renting out a room. The difference is that renting out means you are doing it on a monthly basis while a bed and breakfast is more towards a daily thing.

You also need to provide breakfast for those who stay with you. This works well if you live in a place where tourists frequent. However, this can be difficult if you have children and need to work. It can affect their safety and your time schedule tremendously.

Cleaning Services For Businesses

Many businesses and institutions required individuals who will provide cleaning services at an affordable price after working hours. This is a great business that you can do after work. It is best for those who are willing to put in a few hours each day after work.

Don't think of cleaning as a low-paid industry. If you get a few cleaning jobs, it can be very lucrative. To get these cleaning services, you need to have marketing skills. You need to tell other people that you are providing such services so that they can give you their service.

Final Notes

Making more money is something that many people desire, but few people achieve. The reason for this is because they lack the skills required.

The skills that I'm talking about isn't in how to perform a certain activity. Rather, it is personal skills such as time management, energy management and the power to constantly motivate yourself. If you lack these skills, you must look to develop them.

After you have learned those skills, then only learn those skills required to make more money. This may be learning 'dropshipping skills' if you want to build a dropshipping business. These 'dropshipping skills' might include how to build a website, how to drive traffic and the ability to connect to customers.

Making more money requires discipline because it would be a testing period at the beginning. It may mean sacrificing sleep or time with your children. You would need to put on hold certain activities that you have.

Therefore, you need to hold onto the bigger picture. You need the bigger picture to drive you forward. Think about what your life would be like if you want more money each month.

What if you make an extra $1,000 a month? How much easier would your life be? Would you be able to pay off your debt easily?

Have a vivid picture of the life you would live when you make more money. This would become your motivation in the future. I wish you luck in your money-making endeavor and your life as a single father!

LEAVE A REVIEW

I hope this book has helped you well. It isn't my intention at all to go deep into the topic. I am no expert in everything. However, I have the help of many other single fathers who have shared with me their invaluable experience.

If this book has helped you in any way, do leave me a review. This helps build our single father community.

If you feel that this book can be improved in any way, do mention it in the review. I would love to hear from you.

I wish you luck as a single father…

ABOUT NICK THOMAS

Nicholas Thomas has helped many single fathers cope with divorce in the past few years. By helping them gain more confidence and stability in their lives, he is able to guide them towards being a man that attracts other women easily.

He divorced back in 2008 and knows how difficult a divorce can be for a man. It was a terrible time for him when he got his divorce. He envisioned his children blaming him and not being able to spend time with him. It gave him a constant guilt trip.

Being a divorced man can be very difficult. Ever since his 'emotional recovery' from the divorce, he has helped many single fathers by advising and helping them gain confidence.

Should you want to share your story with him, you can do so at www.singledaddydating.com/shareastory/

ALSO BY NICK THOMAS

(1) Dating After Divorce For The Single Daddy

(2) Dating Ideas For The Single Daddy

(3) How To Be An Alpha Male

(4) First Date Conversations

(5) Online Dating

(6) How To Approach Women

(7) Mature Dating

(8) Single Parent Support

(9) Coping With Divorce

(10) Parenting After Divorce

Visit www.singledaddydating.com/bookstore/

Get Your Complimentary
FREE BOOK

Join our community today and get **10 Crucial Checklist To Dating Success For Single Fathers** FREE, delivered right to your email…

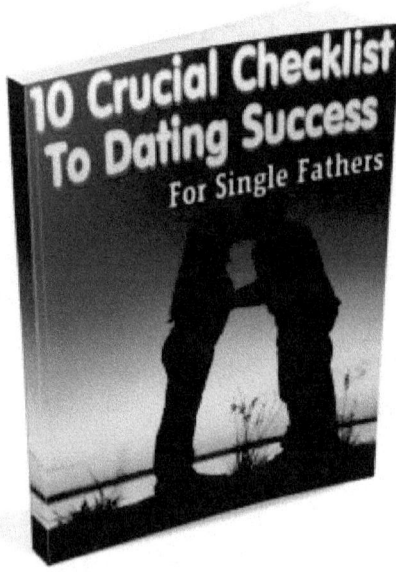

JOIN US AT
WWW.SINGLEDADDYDATING.COM/
NEWSLETTER/

www.ingramcontent.com/pod-product-compliance
Lightning Source LLC
Chambersburg PA
CBHW071810170526
45167CB00003B/1245